Reach
Zero Defects
In Your Software

Empirical Study

Dr. Alfons Unmuessig

ABOAT the AUTHOR

Alfons Unmuessig holds a PhD. in Business Management with a focus on Software-Development and Software-Quality. He has worked many years in upper Management positions e.g. as CEO and Business Unit Leader with worldwide responsibilities of large complex real time Software driven systems.
Bevor this time he has had a position with global responsibilities as Vice President of Quality-Process- and Project-Management.

After his study of Informatics and Business Administration he worked as a Software-Engineer and later on department leader of Software-Development.

Based on his wide theoretical and practical knowledge he is an Author of very-good understanding Software and Quality books

Alfons Unmuessig is a part time Lecturer of 2 Universities.

CONTENTS

Abstract   6

1.   Introduction   8

2.   Objective and Structure of the Study   10
      2.1   Objective   10

      2.2   Structure   11

3.   Sources of Success Criteria   12

4.   List of Success Criteria   17

5.   Expert Interviews   27

6.   Conducting the interviews   30

7.   Results of the Interviews   31

8.   Charts of the main results   33

9.   Graphic Representation of top 15   42

10.   Explantation of Succes Criteria   44

11.   Sumery of Results   50

12.   Conclusion   53

Referenzes

Abstract

The book will help you to produce better Software-Quality

Software defect prevention and software quality have been constantly improved over the past years, e.g. by applying various methods and measures and using modern programming languages.

As the complexity and the scale of the software (SW) that has to designed are continually growing, it is necessary for the software quality to keep in step with this development. However, keeping in step is not enough because software applications are used more and more in security-related areas where e.g. human lives are at risk.

One aspect of a further optimization of SW quality therefore is the determination of the success criteria that lead to a further prevention of errors. This prevention of software errors is especially important in the initial phases of software development.

The following text therefore shows the essential success criteria for reducing errors and consequently further improving SW quality. The author determined these success criteria in an extensive analysis, e.g. by thorough review of relevant literature, results of congresses on SW quality, interviews and considerable own professional experience.

In the interviews with 18 experts in 3 countries, the determined success criteria were assessed regarding their importance, effectiveness and degree of networking. The results are shown in various figures and also explained.

Other analyses of the success criteria will be / have already been published by the author on Amazon.com/.de.

The assessment of the success criteria enables the reader and user of these criteria to set the right priorities for the optimization of SW quality during software development.

Keywords:

Software, Zero-Defects, Software-Development, Empirical-Study, Defect-Prevention, Improve-Software-Quality, Success-Criteria, Practical-Application.

1.   INTRODUCTION

Finding and removing software errors is essential but is becoming more and more expensive and annoys customers. Defect / error prevention in the software development process therefore gains in importance. Defect Prevention is a strategy applied to the software development life cycle that identifies root causes of defects and prevents them from recurring. It is the essence of Total Quality Management (TQM). In general, Defect Prevention activities are a mechanism for propagating the knowledge of lessons learned between projects. It is a real challenge because there is a vast diversity of SW errors, they are hard to detect and finding them is very expensive. SW errors are also often connected with hardware; therefore, the error cause cannot be immediately attributed to the software or the hardware. As software does not wear out, the errors are created in the development process. organizations have an established software process to carry out their responsibilities. This process is enhanced when Defect Prevention methodologies are implemented to improve quality and productivity and reduce development costs. The majority of errors (50-70%) originate in the requirements, specifications and design. The error causes are based on various reasons, e.g. human error or technical reasons. This results in the following questions:

1. Which success criteria (SC) are the most important for defect / error prevention in software development processes ?

2. How strong is the effect of the individual success criteria ?

3. How large is the degree of networking between the success criteria ?

2. OBJECTIVE AND STRUCTURE OF THE STUDY

2.1 OBJECTIVE

The objectives of the study are determining the success criteria (SC) and their effects on error prevention and therefore also on software quality. These SC are essential inputs for the optimization of software quality and error prevention. In the software development process, these criteria are e.g. support by the top management, motivation of the employees, application of maturity models, e.g. CMMI, extensive requirements analysis (see list of success criteria in chapter 3).

Each success criteria is assessed by an expert with regard to its importance, effectiveness and degree of networking, so the reader and user gets clear statements on the relevance of each individual SC for error prevention / software quality.

2.2 STRUCTURE

- **Sources and Determination of the main** ...
success criteria (SC)

- **Interviews with experts regarding the SC**

- **Results & graphic presentation of the study**

- **Summary of the results**

The basis of the success criteria of Software defect prevention is the software development process shown in the following chart and the involved people, the applied methods, tools, the involved units, positions etc.

3. SOURCES OF SUCCESS CRITERIA

The software development process is divided into several phases. The individual phases are defined differently in specialist literature; the definition also depends partly on the chosen procedure model.

The author refers to the following phases (figure 1):

● Phases of Software Development Process

| Requirements-analysis | Design | Implemen-tation | Modul-test | Integration-test | System-test | Field use | Improve-ments |

● Procedure Models for SW Development
- Waterfallmodel, V- Model, V-Model 97
- Spiralmodel
- and others

● Procedure Models describe
- Procedure
- Methods
- Tools-Requirements

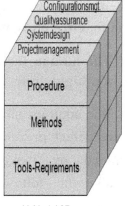

V- Model 97

● Comprehensive Systemic Failure Prevention requests
an new approach/ model

Figure 1: Own illustration; based on Source: Software development process; [Hindel]

The individual phases of the software development process are supported by the project and quality management [Schatten]. They are linked to each other by milestones or are pursued using milestone deadlines.

Error prevention is part of the software development process and therefore has to start in the phase of requirements analysis because this is where a very large part of the errors is caused. As defect prevention should take place in the first three phases **(1. requirements analysis, 2. specification, 3. design)**, the determination of success criteria for error prevention focuses on these 3 phases.

Note: The human factor with all the important success criteria is highly relevant in all eight phases.

Due to the complex situation, the main success criteria for software defect prevention / software quality have to be determined by making a selection and clustering. Especially the following criteria are determined and analyzed:

The following Headline Points from 1 to 6 e.g.

See Headline: <u>4. LIST OF SUCCESS CRITERIA</u>

**1. Human success criteria, e.g.
management, expert knowledge and motivation.**

2. Success criteria from methods of software error prevention, e.g.
> a. Organizational measures, e.g. quality
> management department

b. Constructive measures, e.g. reviews, application of tools
c. Analytic measures, e.g. testing
d. Psychological measures, e.g. stress the importance of the work.

3. Success criteria from error-based methods of applied quality methods and models, e.g.
FMEA (Failure Mode and Effects Analysis)

4. Success criteria from maturity models, e.g. CMMI, Spice

5. Success criteria from other areas, e.g. medicine

6. Other criteria

Those are for example:
- Studies and own professional experience
- Stimuli from other areas, e.g.
- Psychology
- Medicine
- Culture.

Remark:

In the dissertation of the author: *"Ganzheitlich vernetzte Fehlerprävention im Software-Entwicklungsprozess"*, the sources and reasons of all success criteria are explained in detail.

The dissertation with the ISBN 978-3-8440-1188-3 is published by SHAKER Verlag (see also Amazon.de).

- The results of the interviews for each individual success criterion are also listed in very detailed tables in the dissertation.

1.

4. LIST OF SUCCESS CRITERIA

The following 108 success criteria were determined and analyzed by the author.

Abbriviation: *Employees=E; Executive Manager= EM*

4.1 Human success criteria:

1.1.1 Visions and strategies of the executive Manager (EM) for error prevention

1.1.2 Leadership skills of the executive manager(EM) employees

1.1.3 Support of the executive manager (EM) by the top management

1.1.4 Budget for knowledge management and qualification for the EM and the employees

1.1.5 Qualification of employees (EE) by the executive manager (EM)

1.1.6 Resource management 1

1.1.7 Positive attitude of the EM towards error prevention

1.1.8 Inclusion of the customer by the executive manager

1.1.9 Decision-making and responsibility of the executive manager   1)

1.2.1 Employees (EE) understanding the customers requirements

1.2.2 Expert knowledge and experience of the employees (EE)

1.2.3 Method- and process-oriented way of working of the employees (EE)

1.2.4 Experience and cooperation of the team

1.2.5 Individual employee orientation 1)

1.2.6 Inclusion of the customer by the employees team spirit of the employees

1.2.7 Team spirit of the employees

1.2.8 Level of experiences of PSP, TSP and people CMMI of the employees (EE)

1.2.9 Positive attitude of the employees towards error prevention

1.2.9a Level of motivation of the employees

1.3.1 Customers state their requirements consistently, unambiguously and completely

1.3.2 Inclusion of all parties involved on the part of the customer

1.3.3 Number of requirement changes in the course of the project 1)

1.4.1 Personal/private strain

1.4.2 Level of commitment of all parties involved for error prevention (EP)

1.4.3 Systemic skills

1.4.4 Workload of the employees (EE), e.g. due to lack of resources, stress, etc.

1.4.5 Work morale of the employees

1.4.6 Working atmosphere (quality of cooperation)

1.4.7 Behavioral pattern: Parent ego

1.4.8 Behavioral pattern: Adult ego

1.4.9 Level of turnover of executive manager and EE 1)

1.5.1 Individual knowledge acquisition of EM and EE

1.5.2 Willingness to learn of EM and EE

1.5.3 Available time of EM and EE for knowledge acquisition

1.5.4 Application of methods for knowledge acquisition by EM and EE 1)

1.6.1 Cultural sphere with high quality culture

1.6.2 Level of development of the corporate Culture

1.6.3 Level of development of the error culture of EM and EE

1.6.4 Level of development of the quality culture of EM and EE

1.6.5 Level of development of team culture of EM and EE

1.7.1 Communication skills of EM and EE

1.7.2 Regular, open, honest communication and feedback of EM and EE

4.2 Success criteria from methods of software error prevention

2.1.1 Number of intersection points between method, procedural models and tools

2.1.2 Level of consistency of the development phases

2.1.3 Level of harmonization of methods, procedural models, processes and tools

2.2.1 Application of a traditional quality model, e.g. ISO 9000

2.2.2 Application of a maturity model, e.g. CMMI, SPICE

2.2.3 Application of a software quality model, e.g ISO 25000

2.3.1 Application of simulators for knowledge acquisition and knowledge testing

2.3.2 Application of simulators of the planned software (SW)

2.4.1 Application of adaptable methods, models, processes and tools

2.4.2 Level of standardization and suitability of the methods, models, processes, tools

2.4.3 Constant & consistent implementation of the methods, models, processes, tools

2.5.1 Degree of instability of the software

2.5.2 Degree of instability of the used hardware

2.5.3 Degree of complexity of the SW structure

2.6.1 Number of interfaces with legacy systems

2.6.2 Degree of complexity of the application software

2.6.3 Level of time pressure in the phase of SW programming 1)

2.6.4 Level of reutilization of existing SW modules

2.7.1 Level of adjustment of the used HW and application SW

2.7.2 Level of maturity of the HW, methods, procedural models, processes and tools

2.7.3 Level of adjustment of the methods, procedural models, processes and tools

2.7.4 Level of automation of the software programming 1)

4.3 Success criteria from error based methods of applied quality methods and models,

3.1.1 Quality of the workplace design and environment

3.1.2 Quality of the familiar, local environment and culture

3.2.1 Level of support in implementing improvements and alterations

3.2.2 Nomination and support of a 'zero errors promoter' 1)

3.2.3 Implementation of improvement projects as pilot projects 1)

3.3.1 Level of requirements for procedural model/engineering model

3.3.2 Level of requirements concerning the structure of the requirements

3.3.3 Level of the requirements for quality planning

3.3.4 Level of the requirements for guidelines and checklists 1)

3.4.1 Intensity of the individual personnel management

3.4.2 Level of experience utilization

3.4.3 Level of knowledge utilization

3.4.4 Level of the learning organization 1)

3.5.1 Level of definition of roles

3.5.2 Level of process-oriented organizational design

3.5.3 Level of flexible, task- and qualification-oriented team structure

3.5.4 Level of task-oriented team size and communication 1)

3.6.1 Keeping to the project's budget

3.6.2 Level of compliance with the customer requirements

3.6.3 Keeping to the requirements concerning the project quality

3.6.4 Keeping to the project deadlines

3.7.1 Costs of knowledge management

3.7.2 Level of implementation of knowledge management and knowledge generation

4.4 Success criteria from maturity models

4.1.1 Quality of the requirements management

4.1.2 Quality of the requirements analysis

4.1.3 Quality of the specifications

4.1.4 Quality of the plan 1)

4.2.1 Achieved process maturity level

4.3.1 Extent of version management and control

4.4.1 Level of implementation of regular team building

4.4.2 Level of implementation of regular project planning

4.4.3 Level of implementation of regular control

4.4.4 Level of implementation of the management of software sub-contractors

4.5.1 Level of process orientation in the SW and quality management organization

4.5.2 Level of implementation of the company-wide process training

4.5.3 Level of process description of the SW and quality management organization 1)

4.5.4 Level of implementation of process improvements 1)

4.6.1 Learning by mistakes/'lessons learned'

4.6.2 Level of implementation of the goals for product quality and process quality

4.6.3 Monetary and non-monetary incentives for achieving the quality targets

4.7.1 Level of implementation of FMEA

4.7.2 Application of Quality Gates 1)

4.7.3 Level of implementation of quality function deployment application 1)

Note: **The success criteria marked with 1) were not part of the empirical study. They were only mentioned and discussed by the interviewees at the end of the interview.**

5. EXPERT INTERVIES

The main reason for conducting the expert interviews is to establish the experience and interpretations of the experts.

Structure of the interview questionnaire

The guideline for the interview consists of the introduction to the topic and the questionnaire for the interviewee. In the questionnaire, the success criteria are divided into the extended sociotechnical areas human, technology, organization and processes.

Each success criterion in the questionnaire has three main columns, each of which has three sub columns:

First main column:
- **Importance (I)** of the success criterion with three possible levels from 1 to 3 (3 = high importance);

Second main column:
- **Effectiveness (E)** of the success criterion with three possible levels from 1 to 3; (3 = high effectiveness);

Third main column:
- **Degree of networking** (DN) of the success criterion with three possible levels from 1 to 3; (3 = high degree of networking).

In the following, a part of the questionnaire with the different columns is shown.

Part of the questionnaire

For the following success criteria (SC), please mark the applicable boxes with an X.

3 means you strongly agree, 2 means moderate agreement and 1 means you weakly agree.

(The indented SC are subcategories of the above SC in bold type.)

The questionnaire includes all success criteria listed in chapter 3, except for the ones that are marked with 1).

What	Importance of the Success Criteria (SC) 3= highest			Effective-ness of the SC			Degree of networking of the SC		
Success criteria (SC)	1	2	3	1	2	3	1	2	3
HUMAN									
Human as executive manager (EM)									
Visions and strategies of the EM for error prevention									
Leadership skills of the EM									
Support of the EM by the top management									

6. CONDUCTING THE INTERVIEWS

The interviewees did receive an electronic version of the guideline and the questionnaire approx. 2 weeks in advance of the interview to familiarize themselves with the topic. Depending on the requests and the residence of the expert, the interviews were conducted face-to-face, over the telephone, or the expert filled in the questionnaire and sent it back. Out of the 18 interviews in 13 companies, approx. 70% were conducted face-to-face, 20% over the telephone and 10% without direct participation of the author. An interview lasted about 1.5 hours. From CEO to specialist, people from all levels in software development and SW quality management were chosen as interviewees. Sources for finding interviewees were the attendance lists of software development and quality congresses in Europe, e.g. in Bulgaria, Germany, Switzerland, Denmark and Austria, and various companies.

7.   RESULTS OF THE INTERVIEWS

The results were shown in statistical charts, regarding the **importance (I)** of the **success criteria (SC),** their **effectiveness (E)** and their **degree of networking (DN).** The data quality of the experts' assessments is good. The top 15 of the SC for every column were illustrated in the respective chart.

In the **first part of the questionnaire,** the two main questions regarding software error prevention were answered as follows:

Question 1:
Do you think that further optimization of the current methods/models/measures including new approaches for software defect prevention is necessary?
Answer 1:
100% of the experts said: **yes.**

Question 2:
In which area do you see a strong need for action?
Answer 2:

90% of the experts confirmed that there is an **urgent need** for action in the **requirements analysis** and specification; 80% also mentioned the design.

The experts also mentioned other success criteria during/after the interview and the following **additional need for action**: tests, communication with more pictures, modeling right from the beginning, constant knowledge development, constant awareness of problems, more acting on one's own responsibility and accepting responsibility.

In the **second part of the questionnaire**, the extensive questions regarding the **success criteria** (SC) for SW defect prevention were asked.

The respective columns in the **second part** of the questionnaire Importance (I_1, I_2, I_3) as well as **Effectiveness** (E_1, E_2, E_3) and **Degree of Networking** (DN_1, DN_2, DN_3) show the following assessment: 1 means "weak", 2 means "moderate" and 3 means "strong" agreement.

8. CHARTS OF THE MAIN RESULTS

In the following figure 8.1, the columns are analyzed regarding:

a) Importance (I)

- From the boxes to be checked in the **I column** in all questionnaires, 99.24% were marked.
- The success criteria (SC) regarding the importance defined by the author were confirmed with 90.97% ($I_3 + I_2$) because in column C3 = 58.46% (I_3) are marked as very important and in column C2 = 32.51% (I_2) are marked as moderately important.

b) Effectiveness (E)

- From the boxes to be checked in the **E column,** 98.17% were marked.
- The effectiveness of the success criteria was confirmed with 85.47% ($E_3 + E_2$) because in column C3 = 43.09% (E_3) are marked as strong and in column C2 = 42.38% (E_2) are marked as moderate.

c) Degree of Networking (DN)

- From the boxes to be checked in the
- **DN column,** 99.62% were marked.

- The degree of networking is 75.92% (DN_3 + DN_2) because it is marked as strong in column C3 with 32.07% and as moderate in column C2 with 43.85%.

- **Note:** Most of the boxes were filled in; it hardly ever happened that a boxes that had to be marked was not checked.

In the following figure 8.1, the analysis of the three columns importance of the Success Criteria (SC), effectiveness of the SC and degree of networking of the (SC) is shown.

Note: Importance (I$_3$), Effectivness (E$_3$) and Degree of Networking (DN$_3$) stand for the strongest agreement.

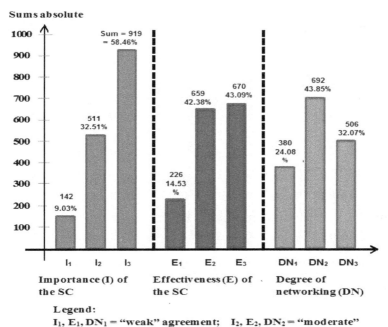

Figure 8.1: Analysis of the columns importance (Ix), effectiveness (Ex) and degree of networking (DNx), absolute and in %; range of x: 1 to 3; [source: own illustration]

Determination/graphic representation of the top 15 for importance (I_3) of the success criteria

In figure 8.2, the ranking of the 15 most significant success criteria (SC) regarding the importance (I_3) is shown.

Note: I_3 is the highest importance.

In the ranking of the Top 15, the success criteria (SC) "1.2.1 Understanding the customers' requirements" comes in **first**.

In **second place**, there is the success criteria (SC) "1.6.4 Level of development of the quality culture of executive manager (EM) and employee (EE)".

The success criteria (SC) "4.1.2 Quality of the requirements analysis" comes in **third**.

The explanation of all success criteria shown in the figures can be found in chapter 6.

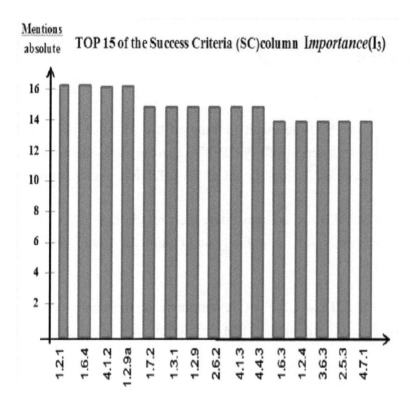

Figure 8.2: TOP 15: Importance (I_3) of the success criteria; [source: own illustration]

1.2.1 Employees (EE) understanding the customers Requirements.

1.6.4 Level of development of the quality culture of Executive Manager and Employees.

4.1.2 Quality of requirements analysis.

1.2.9a Level of motivation of the Employees.

Determination / graphic representation of the top 15 for effectiveness (E₃) of the success criteria (SC)

In figure 8.3, the exact ranking of the 15 most important Success Criteria (SC) (TOP 15) regarding the effectiveness (E_3) (column 3 = main column for effectiveness) is shown.

The SC "1.3.1 Customers state their requirements consistently, unambiguously and completely" is in **first place**.

The SC "1.6.4 Level of development of the quality culture of executive manager (EM) and employee (EE)" comes in **second**.

In **third place**, there is the SC "1.2.1 EE understanding the customers' requirements".

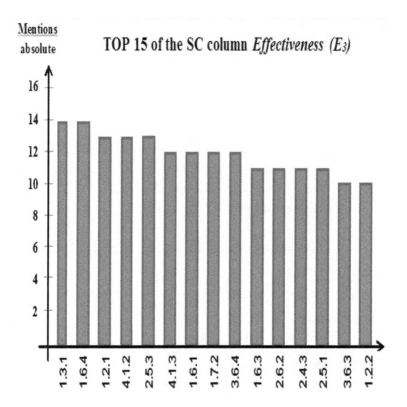

Figure 8.3: TOP 15: Effectiveness (E_3); [source: own illustration]

1.3.1 Customers state their requirements consistenly, unambiguously and completely.

1.6.4 Level of development of the quality culture of Executive Manager and Employees.

1.2.1 Employees (EE) understanding the customers Requirements.

4.1.2 Quality of requirements analysis.

Remaining Success Criteria see Chapter 4

Determination / graphic representation of the top 15 for degree of networking (DN$_3$)

In figure 8.4, the complete ranking of the 15 most frequently mentioned Success Criteria (SC) (TOP 15) with regard to the degree of networking (DN$_3$) (column 3 = main column for degree of networking) is shown.

The SC "4.1.3 Quality of the specifications" has the highest degree of networking, according to the number of mentions, followed by SC "1.6.3 Level of development of the error culture of executive manager (EM) and employee (EE)" and SC "4.4.3 Level of implementation of regular project control".

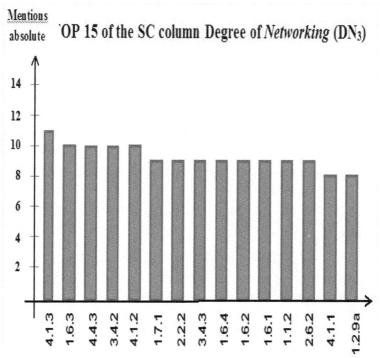

Figure 8.4: Top 15: Degree of Networking (DN$_3$); [source: own illustration]

4.1.3 Quality of the specification.

1.6.3   Level of development of the error culture of Executive Manager and Employees.

4.4.3 Level of implementation of regular control.

3.4.2 Level of experience utilization.

Remaining Success Criteria see Chapter 4

9. Graphic Representation of the top 15

In figure 9.1, the ranking of the most frequently mentioned TOP 15 is shown as a triple of Importance (I_3), Effektivness (E_3) and Degree of Networking) (DN_3). These combinations where the columns I_3, E_3 and DN_3 were marked simultaneously for one success criterion (SC) show that the respective combination was assessed as strong and that its influence on error prevention is significant.

The SC "4.1.2 Quality of the requirements analysis" comes in **first**,
the SC "4.1.3 Quality of the specifications" comes in **second** and
the SC "1.6.4 Level of development of the quality culture of executive manager (EM) and employee (EE)" comes in **third**.

The diagram / results of Figure 5 are very important.

It shows the strongest Success Criterias (SC) as all three columns (Importance (I), Effectiveness (E) and Degree of Networking (DN) have bin marked up to for the selected SC.

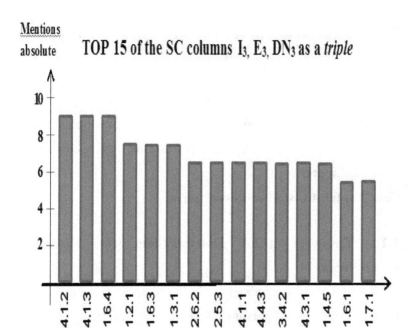

Figure 9.1: Top 15: All three columns (I3, E3, DN3) are marked; [source: own illustration]

4.1.2 Quality of requirements analysis.

4.1.3 Quality of the specification.

1.6.4 Level of development of the quality culture of Executive Manager and Employees.

1.2.1 Employees (EE) understanding the customers Requirements.

Remaining Success Criteria see Chapter 4

10. EXPLANATION OF SUCCES CRITERIA

The following, success criteria shown in the figures are explained. Each success criteria starts with its number e.g. **1.2.1 Employees (EE) understanding the customers requirements.**
See Chapter 4 List of success criteria.

1.2.1 Employee (EE) understanding the customers requirements

Understanding the customers' requirements is a complex task because often two persons/cultures with different ways of thinking are involved in the process. The customers explain their requirements orally or in writing. These are often not completely comprehensible or compatible with those of the supplier or software developer. Customer and supplier often have different educations, thoughts, self-images regarding software requirements, expert/domain knowledge [Hamilton]. Because of that, the customers' requirements can be misinterpreted by the supplier.

In specialist literature, the topic of requirements analysis and management and requirements engineering is described in detail (e.g. Pohl) and is therefore not explained further here.

1.2.4 Experience and cooperation of the team

Software development is teamwork and is based on experience and cooperation.

1.2.9 Positive attitude of the Employee towards error prevention

The attitude towards quality / error prevention is the key point of the Berlin TQM implementation model [see Kamiske 2005, p. 105] and can therefore be seen as decisive.

1.2.9a Level of motivation of the Employee

Motivation can be defined as the reason for a certain human behavior [Strunz]. The motivation is very important for error prevention as it strongly influences the will to avoid errors.

The employees mobilize their energy to reach a certain goal. In this case, the goal is "to prevent errors".

1.3.1 Customers state their requirements consistently, unambiguously and completely

A precise definition of the requirements is the basis for error prevention. If possible, the definition of the requirements should take place in close cooperation between the software supplier (software developers / system specialists) and the customer.

1.4.5 Work morale of the Employee (EE)

A low work morale is detrimental to error prevention as the employees might not see any point in it.

1.6.1 Cultural sphere with high quality culture

In a cultural sphere with a high quality culture, quality awareness is very strong. A company in this cultural sphere has very good prerequisites for a high quality culture and therefore good prerequisites for error prevention.

1.6.3 Level of development of the error culture of Executive Management (EM) and Employee (EE)

According to literature research and own experience, the criterion "error culture" significantly influences SW error prevention. The term "error culture" is strange because "culture" has a positive connotation but "error culture" is negative [Caspary]. For example, if someone produces software errors and freely admits it, he or she is often considered a negligent employee and is therefore checked more frequently. This is not a good error culture because such an error culture includes a positive attitude towards errors that have been made in order to learn from them. Error culture means that we handle errors openly and constructively. The process towards an optimal error culture in a company is long.

1.6.4 Level of development of the quality culture of Executive Management (EM) and Employee (EE)

The quality culture of a company is very important for a successful error prevention as the quality culture resulting from the corporate culture is part of the corporate quality [Seghezzi 1996, p. 181]. Executive managers should set an example of quality and employee responsibility in their everyday work.

1.7.1 Communication skills of EM and EE

The communication between management and employees is a success factor [EXBA], e.g. for discussing the requirements with the customer and understanding them. Statistical studies and analyses have shown that wrong communication or a lack of it lead to misunderstandings, especially in the requirements management [Hamilton].

1.7.2 Regular, open, honest communication and feedback of EM and EE

Communication skills make a regular communication with all involved parties possible. This also includes communication in the case of success [Mc Donald p. 396]. Within the wide range of communication, openness, honesty, the willingness to listen and e.g. confessing software errors without fear are very beneficial.

2.5.3 Degree of complexity of the SW structure

A complex SW structure increases the likelihood of emergent SW errors. The goal is to have a low degree of complexity of the SW structure.

2.6.2 Degree of complexity of the application software

The degree of complexity of the application software influences the error probability.

3.4.2 Level of experience utilization

The experience of each individual employee should be used in the best possible way in the organization. To achieve this, a knowledge data base is used where experience can be entered but also read.

3.6.3 Keeping to the requirements concerning the project quality

In order to prevent errors, requirements concerning the project quality have to be observed.

4.1.1 Quality of the requirements management

The requirements management has the task to cope with the requirements [Pohl p. 626]. More precisely, this means the pursuit, maintenance, administration and coordination of the requirements. They define the qualitative and quantitative SW features from the customer's view.

4.1.2 Quality of the requirements analysis

The requirements analysis is a systematic approach that is indispensable for error prevention in order to see the requirements for the system that has to be created from the customer's view (requirements specification) and to gradually elaborate them.

4.1.3 Quality of the specifications

A specification is a breakdown of the overall system into components. This shows the static structure and the dynamic behavior of the overall system.

4.3.1 Extent of version management and control

Configuration management clearly identifies every creation and modification of work results, e.g. plans, requirements, specifications, designs, different code parts. The identification has to be archived securely and for the long term in a file system [Kneuper p. 49]. Only certain users should be able to access it.

4.4.3 Level of implementation of regular project control

The project status has to be constantly monitored and if deviations occur, measures for correcting them must be taken.

4.7.1 Level of implementation of FMEA

The risk management uses various methods and procedures, e.g. FMEA (Failure Mode and Effects Analysis). The FMEA defines the probability of occurrence of the possible consequences and causes, the measures and the new risk number for each risk element.

11. SUMERY OF RESULTS

Due to the interviews and the analysis of the questionnaires, the empirical study provides important aspects for error prevention and software quality. The interviewees from various software sector and positions in the companies had a very positive attitude towards the topic of integrally networked error prevention.

The high number of success criteria (SC) was a surprise for many interviewees but was nevertheless confirmed with 90.97% (58.46% very important and 32.51% important).

The importance of the human factor was confirmed by the relatively high number (59.01%) of marked answers for I_3 "human".

The four most important top 15 (I_3) Success Criteria (SC) were the following: (each with 16 out of 18 possible mentions)

No. "1.2.1 Employees (EE) understanding the customers' requirements",

No. "1.6.4 Level of development of the quality culture of EM and EE",

No. "4.1.2 Quality of the requirements analysis" and

No. "1.2.9a Level of motivation of the EE".

The two most effective (E_3) SC were No. "1.3.1 Customers state their requirements consistently, unambiguously and completely" and No. "1.6.4 Level of development of the quality culture of EM and EE", each with 14 out of 18 possible mentions.

No. "1.2.1 Understanding the customers' requirements" comes third.

The SC "4.1.3 Quality of the specifications" has the highest degree of networking (DN_3) with 13 out of 18 possible mentions, followed by No. "1.6.3 Level of development of the error culture".

The analysis of the top 15 combinations (triple) of the columns I_3 & E_3 & DN_3 shows the "statistical" influence of the 15 most important SC on error prevention. The SC "4.1.2 Quality of the requirements analysis", "4.1.3 Quality of the specifications" and "1.6.4 Level of development of the quality culture" come in first, second and third.

12. CONCLUSION

It can be concluded from the empirical study, that error prevention is mainly influenced by the human factors and the processes but the areas of technology and organization are also important.

Note: The level of development (stage) of the quality culture plays a decisive part in software defect prevention.

13. REFERENCES

Unmuessig, A. (1) Various e-Books; See AMAZON.com and AMAZON.de

Unmuessig, A. (2) *The Human being as key Element for Software Process Improve- ment;* GRIN Verlag München Germany ISBN: 978-3-656-34475-9;

Unmuessig, A. (3) *Ermittlung & Bewertung der wichtigsten Erfolgskriterien zur Software-Fehlervermeidung;* GRIN Verlag Mün- chen Germany ISBN: 978-3-656-45708-4;

Unmuessig, A. (4) *Ganzheitlich vernetzte Fehler- prävention im Software-Entwicklungs-prozess;* SHAKER Verlag Aachen ISBN: 978-3-8440-1188-3; Dissertation

Unmuessig, A. (5) *Software Defect Prevention for better Software Quality;* GRIN Verlag München Germany ISBN: 978-3-656-20659-0;

Balzert, H.F. *Lehrbuch der Software-Technik;* Software- Management, Software- Qualitätssicherung, Unternehmensmodellierung. Spektrum, Akademischer Verlag Heidelberg/Berlin

Bunse, C./Knethen, A. . Vorgehensmodelle Kompakt; Spektrum Akademischer Verlag Heidelberg

Dörner, D. *Die Logik des Misslingens;* Strategisches Denken in komplexen Situationen; Powohlt Taschenbuch Verlag 7. Auflage

Gabler_a. Gabler online Wirtschaftslexikon

Gerlich, Ra. & Re. *111 Thesen zur erfolgreichen Softwareentwicklung;* Springer Verlag, Berlin/Heidelberg

Gomez, P., Probst, G. *Vernetztes Denken im Management;* Die Orientierung Nr. 89, CH-Bern, Schweizerische Volksbank

Gomez, P., Probst, G. . *Die Praxis des ganzheitlichen Problemlösens;* *V*ernetzt denken, Unternehmerisch handeln, Persönlich überzeugen; 2. überarbeitete Auflage; Bern, Stuttgart, Wien,

Grossmann, C. *Komplexitätsbewältigung im Management;* Anleitungen, integrierte Methodik und Anwendungsbeispiele; Verlag GCN, Winterthur

Hindel, B. **& andere Basiswissen Software-Projektmanagement;** dpunkt Verlag, Heidelberg

Hamilton, P. *Dynaxity*; Management von Dynamik und Komplexität im Softwarebau; Springer Verlag Berlin Heidelberg

Hamilton, P. . *Wege aus der Softwarekrise;* Springer Verlag Berlin Heidelberg

Hörmann, K./Dittmann, L./Hindel, B. *SPICE in der Praxis;* Interpretationshilfe für Anwender und Assessoren, basierend auf ISO/IEC 15504, dpunkt.Verlag, Heidelberg

Hoffman, D. W. *Software Qualität;* Springer-Verlag, Berlin Heidelberg

Kamiske, G. F.. *Qualitäts-Wissenschaftliches Manager-Handbuch;* Verlag Lehmanns Media-LOB.de Berlin, Germany. ISBN 3-86541-067-7.

Kneuper, R. *CMMI Verbesserung von Softwareprozessen mit Capability Maturity Model Integration;* 2. überarbeitete und erweiterte Auflage, Verlag dpunkt.verlag, Heidelberg, Germany. ISBN 3-89864-373-5.

McDonald, M.. Musson, R.; Smith, R; *The Practical Guide to Defect Prevention;* Techniques to Meet the Demand for More Reliable Software; Microsoft Press; Redmond, Wa, USA. ISBN 978-07356-2253-1.

Masing, W. *Handbuch Qualitätsmanagement;* Herausgegeben von T. Pfeifer/R. Schmitt, 5., vollständig neu bearbeitete Auflage, Hanser Verlag München

Pohl, K. . *Requirements Engineering;* Grundlagen, Prinzipien, Techniken; 2., korrigierte Auflage dpunkt. Verlag Heidelberg, Germany. ISBN 978-3-89864-550-8.

Reason, I. . *Human Error*; Cambridge University Press New York, USA

Schatten, A. und andere : *Best Practise Software-Engineering;* Spektrum Akademischer Verlag Heidelberg, Germany. ISBN 978-3827424860.

Schein, E.H. *Organisationskultur;* The Ed Schein Corporate Culture Survival Guide; MIT/Cambridge USA; Edition Humanistische Psychologie, Bergisch Gladbach

Seghezzi, H. D. *Integriertes Qualitätsmanagement;* Das St. Galler Konzept München; Hanser Verlag München

Seghezzi, H.D. *Integriertes Qualitätsmanagement;* Der St. Galler Ansatz; 3. völlig überarbeitete Auflage; Hanser Verlag München

Senge, P. *Die fünfte Disziplin;* Die Kunst und Praxis der Lernenden Organisation; Schöffer-Poeschel, 10. Auflage

Strunz, H. Dorsch, M. *Management;* Managementwissen für Studium und Praxis, Oldenburg Wissenschaftsverlag München

Vester, F. *Die Kunst vernetzt zu denken;* Ideen und Werkzeuge für einen neuen Umgang mit Komplexität, 6. Auflage, dtv Verlag, München

Wallmüller, E. . *Software Qualitätsmanagement in der Praxis;* 2., völlig überarbeitete Auflage, Hanser Verlag München